A problem well put is half-solved. The reactionary is a man of few words, well-chosen, which cut to the heart of a problem. In the history of ideas there have been works which have laid bare the problems of modernity, and whose elegance has pointed the way to their solution.

Imperium Press' Studies in Reaction series distills the essence of reactionary thought. The series presents in compact format those seminal works which need so few words to say so much about modernity.

HAVAMAL
&
NORSE PROVERBS

PERTH
IMPERIUM PRESS
2022

Published by Imperium Press

www.imperiumpress.org

Poetic Edda published by the
American-Scandinavian Foundation 1923

FIRST EDITION

A catalogue record for this
book is available from the
National Library of Australia

ISBN 978-1-922602-54-1 Paperback
ISBN 978-1-922602-55-8 E-book

CONTENTS

HAVAMAL
&
NORSE PROVERBS

1   Within the gates ere a man shall go,
Full warily let him watch,
Full long let him look about him;
For little he knows where a foe may lurk,
And sit in the seats within.

2   Hail to the giver! a guest has come;
Where shall the stranger sit?
Swift shall he be who, with swords shall try
The proof of his might to make.

3   Fire he needs who with frozen knees
Has come from the cold without;
Food and clothes must the farer have,
The man from the mountains come.

4   Water and towels and welcoming speech
Should he find who comes, to the feast;
If renown he would get, and again be greeted,
Wisely and well must he act.

5   Wits must he have who wanders wide,
But all is easy at home;
At the witless man the wise shall wink
When among such men he sits.

6   A man shall not boast of his keenness of
      mind,
But keep it close in his breast;
To the silent and wise does ill come seldom
When he goes as guest to a house;
For a faster friend one never finds
Than wisdom tried and true.

7   The knowing guest who goes to the feast,
In silent attention sits;
With his ears he hears, with his eyes he
      watches,
Thus wary are wise men all.

8   Happy the one who wins for himself
Favor and praises fair;
Less safe by far is the wisdom found
That is hid in another's heart.

9   Happy the man who has while he lives
Wisdom and praise as well,
For evil counsel a man full oft
Has from another's heart.

10   A better burden may no man bear
For wanderings wide than wisdom;
It is better than wealth on unknown ways,
And in grief a refuge it gives.

11   A better burden may no man bear
For wanderings wide than wisdom;
Worse food for the journey he brings not
      afield
Than an over-drinking of ale.

12   Less good there lies than most believe
In ale for mortal men;
For the more he drinks the less does man
Of his mind the mastery hold.

13   Over beer the bird of forgetfulness broods,
And steals the minds of men;
With the heron's feathers fettered I lay
And in Gunnloth's house was held.

14   Drunk I was, I was dead-drunk,
When with Fjalar wise I was;
'Tis the best of drinking if back one brings
His wisdom with him home.

15   The son of a king shall be silent and wise,
And bold in battle as well;
Bravely and gladly a man shall go,
Till the day of his death is come.

16   The sluggard believes he shall live forever,
If the fight he faces not;
But age shall not grant him the gift of peace,
Though spears may spare his life.

17   The fool is agape when he comes to the feast,
He stammers or else is still;
But soon if he gets a drink is it seen
What the mind of the man is like.

18   He alone is aware who has wandered wide,
And far abroad has fared,
How great a mind is guided by him
That wealth of wisdom has.

19 Shun not the mead, but drink in measure;
   Speak to the point or be still;
   For rudeness none shall rightly blame thee
   If soon thy bed thou seekest.

20 The greedy man, if his mind be vague,
   Will eat till sick he is;
   The vulgar man, when among the wise,
   To scorn by his belly is brought.

21 The herds know well when home they shall
      fare,
   And then from the grass they go;
   But the foolish man his belly's measure
   Shall never know aright.

22 A paltry man and poor of mind
   At all things ever mocks;
   For never he knows, what he ought to know,
   That he is not free from faults.

23 The witless man is awake all night,
   Thinking of many things;
   Care-worn he is when the morning comes,
   And his woe is just as it was.

24 The foolish man for friends all those
   Who laugh at him will hold;
   When among the wise he marks it not
   Though hatred of him they speak.

25   The foolish man for friends all those
Who laugh at him will hold;
But the truth when he comes to the council
  he learns,
That few in his favor will speak.

26   An ignorant man thinks that all he knows,
When he sits by himself in a corner;
But never what answer to make he knows,
When others with questions come.

27   A witless man, when he meets with men,
Had best in silence abide;
For no one shall find that nothing he knows,
If his mouth is not open too much.
But a man knows not, if nothing he knows,
When his mouth has been open too much.

28   Wise shall he seem who well can question,
And also answer well;
Nought is concealed that men may say
Among the sons of men.

29   Often he speaks who never is still
With words that win no faith;
The babbling tongue, if a bridle it find not,
Oft for itself sings ill.

30   In mockery no one a man shall hold,
Although he fare to the feast;
Wise seems one oft, if nought he is asked,
And safely he sits dry-skinned.

31   Wise a guest holds it to take to his heels,
      When mock of another he makes;
      But little he knows who laughs at the feast,
      Though he mocks in the midst of his foes.

32   Friendly of mind are many men,
      Till feasting they mock at their friends;
      To mankind a bane must it ever be
      When guests together strive.

33   Oft should one make an early meal,
      Nor fasting come to the feast;
      Else he sits and chews as if he would choke,
      And little is able to ask.

34   Crooked and far is the road to a foe,
      Though his house on the highway be;
      But wide and straight is the way to a friend,
      Though far away he fare.

35   Forth shall one go, nor stay as a guest
      In a single spot forever;
      Love becomes loathing if long one sits
      By the hearth in another's home.

36   Better a house, though a hut it be,
      A man is master at home;
      A pair of goats and a patched-up roof
      Are better far than begging.

37   Better a house, though a hut it be,
A man is master at home;
His heart is bleeding who needs must beg
When food he fain[1] would have.

38   Away from his arms in the open field
A man should fare not a foot;
For never he knows when the need for a spear
Shall arise on the distant road.

39   If wealth a man has won for himself,
Let him never suffer in need;
Oft he saves for a foe what he plans for a
   friend,
For much goes worse than we wish.

40   None so free with gifts or food have I found
That gladly he took not a gift,
Nor one who so widely scattered his wealth
That of recompense hatred he had.

41   Friends shall gladden each other with arms
   and garments,
As each for himself can see;
Gift-givers' friendships are longest found,
If fair their fates may be.

42   To his friend a man a friend shall prove,
And gifts with gifts requite;
But men shall mocking with mockery an-
   swer,
And fraud with falsehood meet.

1 Gladly.

43   To his friend a man a friend shall prove,
    To him and the friend of his friend;
    But never a man shall friendship make
    With one of his foeman's friends.

44   If a friend thou hast whom thou fully wilt
      trust,
    And good from him wouldst get,
    Thy thoughts with his mingle, and gifts shalt
      thou make,
    And fare to find him oft.

45   If another thou hast whom thou hardly wilt
      trust,
    Yet good from him wouldst get,
    Thou shalt speak him fair, but falsely think,
    And fraud with falsehood requite.

46   So is it with him whom thou hardly wilt
      trust,
    And whose mind thou mayst not know;
    Laugh with him mayst thou, but speak not
      thy mind,
    Like gifts to his shalt thou give.

47   Young was I once, and wandered alone,
    And nought of the road I knew;
    Rich did I feel when a comrade I found,
    For man is man's delight.

48   The lives of the brave and noble are best,
    Sorrows they seldom feed;
    But the coward fear of all things feels,
    And not gladly the niggard gives.

49   My garments once in a field I gave
To a pair of carven poles;
Heroes they seemed when clothes they had,
But the naked man is nought.

50   On the hillside drear the fir-tree dies,
All bootless its needles and bark;
It is like a man whom no one loves—
Why should his life be long?

51   Hotter than fire between false friends
Does friendship five days burn;
When the sixth day comes the fire cools,
And ended is all the love.

52   No great thing needs a man to give,
Oft little will purchase praise;
With half a loaf and a half-filled cup
A friend full fast I made.

53   A little sand has a little sea,
And small are the minds of men;
Though all men are not equal in wisdom,
Yet half-wise only are all.

54   A measure of wisdom each man shall have,
But never too much let him know;
The fairest lives do those men live
Whose wisdom wide has grown.

55   A measure of wisdom each man shall have,
But never too much let him know;
For the wise man's heart is seldom happy,
If wisdom too great he has won.

56 A measure of wisdom each man shall have,
But never too much let him know;
Let no man the fate before him see,
For so is he freest from sorrow.

57 A brand from a brand is kindled and burned,
And fire from fire begotten;
And man by his speech is known to men,
And the stupid by their stillness.

58 He must early go forth who fain the blood
Or the goods of another would get;
The wolf that lies idle shall win little meat,
Or the sleeping man success.

59 He must early go forth whose workers are
few,
Himself his work to seek;
Much remains undone for the morn-
ing-sleeper,
For the swift is wealth half won.

60 Of seasoned shingles and strips of bark
For the thatch let one know his need,
And how much of wood he must have for a
month,
Or in half a year he will use.

61 Washed and fed to the council fare,
But care not too much for thy clothes;
Let none be ashamed of his shoes and hose,
Less still of the steed he rides,
Though poor be the horse he has.

62 When the eagle comes to the ancient sea,
   He snaps and hangs his head;
   So is a man in the midst of a throng,
   Who few to speak for him finds.

63 To question and answer must all be ready
   Who wish to be known as wise;
   Tell one thy thoughts, but beware of two—
   All know what is known to three.

64 The man who is prudent a measured use
   Of the might he has will make;
   He finds when among the brave he fares
   That the boldest he may not be.

65 [...]
   Oft for the words that to others one speaks
   He will get but an evil gift.

66 Too early to many a meeting I came,
   And some too late have I sought;
   The beer was all drunk, or not yet brewed;
   Little the loathed man finds.

67 To their homes men would bid me hither
      and yon,
   If at meal-time I needed no meat,
   Or would hang two hams in my true friend's
      house,
   Where only one I had eaten.

68   Fire for men is the fairest gift,
      And power to see the sun;
      Health as well, if a man may have it,
      And a life not stained with sin.

69   All wretched is no man, though never so sick;
      Some from their sons have joy,
      Some win it from kinsmen, and some from
        their wealth,
      And some from worthy works.

70   It is better to live than to lie a corpse,
      The live man catches the cow;
      I saw flames rise for the rich man's pyre,
      And before his door he lay dead.

71   The lame rides a horse, the handless is herds-
        man,
      The deaf in battle is bold;
      The blind man is better than one that is
        burned,
      No good can come of a corpse.

72   A son is better, though late he be born,
      And his father to death have fared;
      Memory-stones seldom stand by the road
      Save when kinsman honors his kin.

73   Two make a battle, the tongue slays the head;
      In each furry coat a fist I look for.

74   He welcomes the night whose fare is enough,
       Short are the yards of a ship,
       Uneasy are autumn nights;
       Full oft does the weather change in a week,
       And more in a month's time.

75   A man knows not, if nothing he knows,
       That gold oft apes begets;
       One man is wealthy and one is poor,
       Yet scorn for him none should know.

76   Among Fitjung's sons saw I well-stocked
           folds—
       Now bear they the beggar's staff;
       Wealth is as swift as a winking eye,
       Of friends the falsest it is.

77   Cattle die, and kinsmen die,
       And so one dies one's self;
       But a noble name will never die,
       If good renown one gets.

78   Cattle die, and kinsmen die,
       And so one dies one's self;
       One thing now that never dies,
       The fame of a dead man's deeds.

79   Certain is that which is sought from runes,
       That the gods so great have made,
       And the Master-Poet painted;
       […] of the race of gods:
       Silence is safest and best.

80 An unwise man, if a maiden's love
   Or wealth he chances to win,
   His pride will wax, but his wisdom never,
   Straight forward he fares in conceit.

81 Give praise to the day at evening,
   To a woman on her pyre,
   To a weapon which is tried, to a maid at wed
      lock,
   To ice when it is crossed, to ale that is drunk.

82 When the gale blows hew wood, in fair winds
      seek the water;
   Sport with maidens at dusk, for day's eyes are
      many;
   From the ship seek swiftness, from the shield
      protection,
   Cuts from the sword, from the maiden kisses.

83 By the fire drink ale, over ice go on skates;
   Buy a steed that is lean, and a sword when
      tarnished,
   The horse at home fatten, the hound in thy
      dwelling.

84 A man shall trust not the oath of a maid,
   Nor the word a woman speaks;
   For their hearts on a whirling wheel were
      fashioned,
   And fickle their breasts were formed.

85 In a breaking bow or a burning flame,
   A ravening wolf or a croaking raven,
   In a grunting boar, a tree with roots broken,
   In billowy seas or a bubbling kettle,

86 In a flying arrow or falling waters,
   In ice new formed or the serpent's folds,
   In a bride's bed-speech or a broken sword,
   In the sport of bears or in sons of kings,

87 In a calf that is sick or a stubborn thrall,[2]
   A flattering witch or a foe new slain.

88 In a brother's slayer, if thou meet him abroad,
   In a half-burned house, in a horse full swift—
   One leg is hurt and the horse is useless—
   None had ever such faith as to trust in them
      all.

89 Hope not too surely for early harvest,
   Nor trust too soon in thy son;
   The field needs good weather, the son needs
      wisdom,
   And oft is either denied.

90 The love of women fickle of will
   Is like starting o'er ice with a steed unshod,
   A two-year-old restive and little tamed,
   Or steering a rudderless ship in a storm,
   Or, lame, hunting reindeer on slippery rocks.

2 Slave.

91   Clear now will I speak, for I know them both,
      Men false to women are found;
      When fairest we speak, then falsest we think,
      Against wisdom we work with deceit.

92   Soft words shall he speak and wealth shall
        he offer
      Who longs for a maiden's love,
      And the beauty praise of the maiden bright;
      He wins whose wooing is best.

93   Fault for loving let no man find
      Ever with any other;
      Oft the wise are fettered, where fools go free,
      By beauty that breeds desire.

94   Fault with another let no man find
      For what touches many a man;
      Wise men oft into witless fools
      Are made by mighty love.

95   The head alone knows what dwells near the
        heart,
      A man knows his mind alone;
      No sickness is worse to one who is wise
      Than to lack the longed-for joy.

96   This found I myself, when I sat in the reeds,
      And long my love awaited;
      As my life the maiden wise I loved,
      Yet her I never had.

97 Billing's daughter I found on her bed,
In slumber bright as the sun;
Empty appeared an earl's estate
Without that form so fair.

98 "Othin, again at evening come,
If a woman thou wouldst win;
Evil it were if others than we
Should know of such a sin."

99 Away I hastened, hoping for joy,
And careless of counsel wise;
Well I believed that soon I should win
Measureless joy with the maid.

100 So came I next when night it was,
The warriors all were awake;
With burning lights and waving brands
I learned my luckless way.

101 At morning then, when once more I came,
And all were sleeping still,
A dog found in the fair one's place,
Bound there upon her bed.

102 Many fair maids, if a man but tries them,
False to a lover are found;
That did I learn when I longed to gain
With wiles the maiden wise;
Foul scorn was my meed from the crafty
    maid,
And nought from the woman I won.

103 Though glad at home, and merry with guests,
  A man shall be wary and wise;
  The sage and shrewd, wide wisdom seeking,
  Must see that his speech be fair;
  A fool is he named who nought can say,
  For such is the way of the witless.

104 I found the old giant, now back have I fared,
  Small gain from silence I got;
  Full many a word, my will to get,
  I spoke in Suttung's hall.

105 The mouth of Rati made room for my pas-
    sage,
  And space in the stone he gnawed;
  Above and below the giants' paths lay,
  So rashly I risked my head.

106 Gunnloth gave on a golden stool
  A drink of the marvelous mead;
  A harsh reward did I let her have
  For her heroic heart,
  And her spirit troubled sore.

107 The well-earned beauty well I enjoyed,
  Little the wise man lacks;
  So Othrörir now has up been brought
  To the midst of the men of earth.

108 Hardly, methinks, would I home have come,
  And left the giants' land,
  Had not Gunnloth helped me, the maiden
    good,
  Whose arms about me had been.

109 The day that followed, the frost-giants came,
Some word of Hor to win,
And into the hall of Hor;
Of Bolverk they asked, were he back midst
    the gods,
Or had Suttung slain him there?

110 On his ring swore Othin the oath, methinks;
Who now his troth[3] shall trust?
Suttung's betrayal he sought with drink,
And Gunnloth to grief he left.

111 It is time to chant from the chanter's stool;
By the wells of Urth I was,
I saw and was silent, I saw and thought,
And heard the speech of Hor.
Of runes heard I words, nor were counsels
    wanting,
At the hall of Hor,
In the hall of Hor;
Such was the speech I heard.

112 I rede[4] thee, Loddfafnir! and hear thou my
    rede—
Profit thou hast if thou hearest,
Great thy gain if thou learnest:
Rise not at night, save if news thou seekest,
Or fain to the outhouse wouldst fare.

---

3 Loyalty.
4 Counsel.

113 I rede thee, Loddfafnir! and hear thou my
   rede—
   Profit thou hast if thou hearest,
   Great thy gain if thou learnest:
   Beware of sleep on a witch's bosom,
   Nor let her limbs ensnare thee.

114 Such is her might that thou hast no mind
   For the council or meeting of men;
   Meat thou hatest, joy thou hast not,
   And sadly to slumber thou farest.

115 I rede thee, Loddfafnir! and hear thou my
   rede—
   Profit thou hast if thou hearest,
   Great thy gain if thou learnest:
   Seek never to win the wife of another,
   Or long for her secret love.

116 I rede thee, Loddfafnir! and hear thou my
   rede—
   Profit thou hast if thou hearest,
   Great thy gain if thou learnest:
   If o'er mountains or gulfs thou fain wouldst
   go,
   Look well to thy food for the way.

117 I rede thee, Loddfafnir! and hear thou my
    rede—
    Profit thou hast if thou hearest,
    Great thy gain if thou learnest:
    An evil man thou must not let
    Bring aught of ill to thee;
    For an evil man will never make
    Reward for a worthy thought.

118 I saw a man who was wounded sore
    By an evil woman's word;
    A lying tongue his death-blow launched,
    And no word of truth there was.

119 I rede thee, Loddfafnir! and hear thou my
    rede—
    Profit thou hast if thou hearest,
    Great thy gain if thou learnest:
    If a friend thou hast whom thou fully wilt
    trust,
    Then fare to find him oft;
    For brambles grow and waving grass
    On the rarely trodden road.

120 I rede thee, Loddfafnir! and hear thou my
    rede—
    Profit thou hast if thou hearest,
    Great thy gain if thou learnest:
    A good man find to hold in friendship,
    And give heed to his healing charms.

121 I rede thee, Loddfafnir! and hear thou my
     rede—
     Profit thou hast if thou hearest,
     Great thy gain if thou learnest:
     Be never the first to break with thy friend
     The bond that holds you both;
     Care eats the heart if thou canst not speak
     To another all thy thought.

122 I rede thee, Loddfafnir! and hear thou my
     rede—
     Profit thou hast if thou hearest,
     Great thy gain if thou learnest:
     Exchange of words with a witless ape
     Thou must not ever make.

123 For never thou mayst from an evil man
     A good requital get;
     But a good man oft the greatest love
     Through words of praise will win thee.

124 Mingled is love when a man can speak
     To another all his thought;
     Nought is so bad as false to be,
     No friend speaks only fair.

125 I rede thee, Loddfafnir! and hear thou my
     rede—
     Profit thou hast if thou hearest,
     Great thy gain if thou learnest:
     With a worse man speak not three words in
     dispute,
     Ill fares the better oft
     When the worse man wields a sword.

126   I rede thee, Loddfafnir! and hear thou my
       rede—
    Profit thou hast if thou hearest,
    Great thy gain if thou learnest:
    A shoemaker be, or a maker of shafts,
    For only thy single self;
    If the shoe is ill made, or the shaft prove false,
    Then evil of thee men think.

127   I rede thee, Loddfafnir! and hear thou my
       rede—
    Profit thou hast if thou hearest,
    Great thy gain if thou learnest:
    If evil thou knowest, as evil proclaim it,
    And make no friendship with foes.

128   I rede thee, Loddfafnir! and hear thou my
       rede,
    Profit thou hast if thou hearest,
    Great thy gain if thou learnest:
    In evil never joy shalt thou know,
    But glad the good shall make thee.

129   I rede thee, Loddfafnir! and hear thou my
       rede—
    Profit thou hast if thou hearest,
    Great thy gain if thou learnest:
    Look not up when the battle is on—
    Like madmen the sons of men become—
    Lest men bewitch thy wits.

130 I rede thee, Loddfafnir! and hear thou my
      rede—
   Profit thou hast if thou hearest,
   Great thy gain if thou learnest:
   If thou fain wouldst win a woman's love,
   And gladness get from her,
   Fair be thy promise and well fulfilled;
   None loathes what good he gets.

131 I rede thee, Loddfafnir! and hear thou my
      rede—
   Profit thou hast if thou hearest,
   Great thy gain if thou learnest:
   I bid thee be wary, but be not fearful;
   Beware most with ale or another's wife,
   And third beware lest a thief outwit thee.

132 I rede thee, Loddfafnir! and hear thou my
      rede—
   Profit thou hast if thou hearest,
   Great thy gain if thou learnest:
   Scorn or mocking ne'er shalt thou make
   Of a guest or a journey-goer.

133 Oft scarcely he knows who sits in the house
   What kind is the man who comes;
   None so good is found that faults he has not,
   Nor so wicked that nought he is worth.

134 I rede thee, Loddfafnir! and hear thou my
       rede—
    Profit thou hast if thou hearest,
    Great thy gain if thou learnest:
    Scorn not ever the gray-haired singer,
    Oft do the old speak good;
    Oft from shrivelled skin come skillful coun-
       sels,
    Though it hang with the hides,
    And flap with the pelts,
    And is blown with the bellies.

135 I rede thee, Loddfafnir! and hear thou my
       rede—
    Profit thou hast if thou hearest,
    Great thy gain if thou learnest:
    Curse not thy guest, nor show him thy gate,
    Deal well with a man in want.

136 Strong is the beam that raised must be
    To give an entrance to all;
    Give it a ring, or grim will be
    The wish it would work on thee.

137 I rede thee, Loddfafnir! and hear thou my
 rede—
 Profit thou hast if thou hearest,
 Great thy gain if thou learnest:
 When ale thou drinkest seek might of earth,
 For earth cures drink, and fire cures ills,
 The oak cures tightness, the ear cures magic,
 Rye cures rupture, the moon cures rage,
 Grass cures the scab, and runes the sword-
 cut;
 The field absorbs the flood.

138 I ween that I hung on the windy tree,
 Hung there for nights full nine;
 With the spear I was wounded, and offered
 I was
 To Othin, myself to myself,
 On the tree that none may ever know
 What root beneath it runs.

139 None made me happy with loaf or horn,
 And there below I looked;
 I took up the runes, shrieking I took them,
 And forthwith back I fell.

140 Nine mighty songs I got from the son
 Of Bolthorn, Bestla's father;
 And a drink I got of the goodly mead
 Poured out from Othrörir.

141 Then began I to thrive, and wisdom to get,
 I grew and well I was;
 Each word led me on to another word,
 Each deed to another deed.

142   Runes shalt thou find, and fateful signs,
That the king of singers colored,
And the mighty gods have made;
Full strong the signs, full mighty the signs
That the ruler of gods doth write.

143   Othin for the gods, Dain for the elves,
And Dvalin for the dwarfs,
Alsvith for giants and all mankind,
And some myself I wrote.

144   Knowest how one shall write, knowest how
one shall rede?
Knowest how one shall tint,[5] knowest how
one makes trial?
Knowest how one shall ask, knowest how
one shall offer?
Knowest how one shall send, knowest how
one shall sacrifice?

145   Better no prayer than too big an offering,
By thy getting measure thy gift;
Better is none than too big a sacrifice,
[…]
So Thund of old wrote ere man's race began,
Where he rose on high when home he came.

146   The songs I know that king's wives know not,
Nor men that are sons of men;
The first is called help, and help it can bring
thee
In sorrow and pain and sickness.

5 Paint.

147 A second I know, that men shall need
Who leechcraft long to use;
[...]

148 A third I know, if great is my need
Of fetters to hold my foe;
Blunt do I make mine enemy's blade,
Nor bites his sword or staff.

149 A fourth I know, if men shall fasten
Bonds on my bended legs;
So great is the charm that forth I may go,
The fetters spring from my feet,
Broken the bonds from my hands.

150 A fifth I know, if I see from afar
An arrow fly 'gainst the folk;
It flies not so swift that I stop it not,
If ever my eyes behold it.

151 A sixth I know, if harm one seeks
With a sapling's roots to send me;
The hero himself who wreaks his hate
Shall taste the ill ere I.

152 A seventh I know, if I see in flames
The hall o'er my comrades' heads;
It burns not so wide that I will not quench it,
I know that song to sing.

153 An eighth I know, that is to all
Of greatest good to learn;
When hatred grows among heroes' sons,
I soon can set it right.

154 A ninth I know, if need there comes
     To shelter my ship on the flood;
     The wind I calm upon the waves,
     And the sea I put to sleep.

155 A tenth I know, what time I see
     House-riders flying on high;
     So can I work that wildly they go,
     Showing their true shapes,
     Hence to their own homes.

156 An eleventh I know, if needs I must lead
     To the fight my long-loved friends;
     I sing in the shields, and in strength they go
     Whole to the field of fight,
     Whole from the field of fight,
     And whole they come thence home.

157 A twelfth I know, if high on a tree
     I see a hanged man swing;
     So do I write and color the runes
     That forth he fares,
     And to me talks.

158 A thirteenth I know, if a thane full young
     With water I sprinkle well;
     He shall not fall, though he fares mid the
       host,
     Nor sink beneath the swords.

159 A fourteenth I know, if fain I would name
     To men the mighty gods;
     All know I well of the gods and elves,
     Few be the fools know this.

160 A fifteenth I know, that before the doors
　　Of Delling sang Thjothrörir the dwarf;
　　Might he sang for the gods, and glory for
　　　elves,
　　And wisdom for Hroptatyr wise.

161 A sixteenth I know, if I seek delight
　　To win from a maiden wise;
　　The mind I turn of the white-armed maid,
　　And thus change all her thoughts.

162 A seventeenth I know, so that seldom shall
　　　go
　　A maiden young from me;
　　[...]

163 Long these songs thou shalt, Loddfafnir,
　　Seek in vain to sing;
　　Yet good it were if thou mightest get them,
　　Well, if thou wouldst them learn,
　　Help, if thou hadst them.

164 An eighteenth I know, that ne'er will I tell
　　To maiden or wife of man—
　　The best is what none but one's self doth
　　　know,
　　So comes the end of the songs—
　　Save only to her in whose arms I lie,
　　Or who else my sister is.

165 Now are Hor's words spoken in the hall,
     Kind for the kindred of men,
     Cursed for the kindred of giants:
     Hail to the speaker, and to him who learns!
     Profit be his who has them!
     Hail to them who hearken!

Sigrdrifumol

22 Then first I rede[1] thee, that free of guilt
    Toward kinsmen ever thou art;
    No vengeance have, though they work thee
       harm,
    Reward after death thou shalt win.

23 Then second I rede thee, to swear no oath
    If true thou knowest it not;
    Bitter the fate of the breaker of troth,[2]
    And poor is the wolf of his word.

24 Then third I rede thee, that thou at the Thing[3]
    Shalt fight not in words with fools;
    For the man unwise a worser word
    Than he thinks doth utter oft.

1 Counsel.
2 Loyalty.
3 Governing assembly.

25   Ill it is if silent thou art,
A coward born men call thee,
And truth mayhap they tell;
Seldom safe is fame,
Unless wide renown be won;
On the day thereafter send him to death,
Let him pay the price of his lies.

26   Then fourth I rede thee, if thou shalt find
A wily witch on thy road,
It is better to go than her guest to be,
Though night enfold thee fast.

27   Eyes that see need the sons of men
Who fight in battle fierce;
Oft witches evil sit by the way,
Who blade and courage blunt.

28   Then fifth I rede thee, though maidens fair
Thou seest on benches sitting,
Let the silver of kinship not rob thee of sleep,
And the kissing of women beware.

29   Then sixth I rede thee, if men shall wrangle,
And ale-talk rise to wrath,
No words with a drunken warrior have,
For wine steals many men's wits.

30   Brawls and ale full oft have been
An ill to many a man,
Death for some, and sorrow for some;
Full many the woes of men.

31   Then seventh I rede thee, if battle thou seek-
        est
      With a foe that is full of might;
      It is better to fight than to burn alive
      In the hall of the hero rich.

32   Then eighth I rede thee, that evil thou shun,
      And beware of lying words;
      Take not a maid, nor the wife of a man,
      Nor lure them on to lust.

33   Then ninth I rede thee: burial render
      If thou findest a fallen corpse,
      Of sickness dead, or dead in the sea,
      Or dead of weapons' wounds.

34   A bath shalt thou give them who corpses be,
      And hands and head shalt wash;
      Wipe them and comb, ere they go in the cof-
        fin,
      And pray that they sleep in peace.

35   Then tenth I rede thee, that never thou trust
      The word of the race of wolves,
      If his brother thou broughtest to death,
      Or his father thou didst fell;
      Often a wolf in a son there is,
      Though gold he gladly takes.

36   Battle and hate and harm, methinks,
      Full seldom fall asleep;
      Wits and weapons the warrior needs
      If boldest of men he would be.

37 Then eleventh I rede thee, that wrath thou
         shun,
    And treachery false with thy friends;
    Not long the leader's life shall be,
    For great are the foes he faces.

Reginsmol

They sailed to the land, and the man went on board
the ship, and the storm subsided.

19 Sigurth spake:
    Hnikar, say, for thou seest the fate
    That to gods and men is given;
    What sign is fairest for him who fights,
    And best for the swinging of swords?

20 *Hnikar spake:*
    Many the signs, if men but knew,
    That are good for the swinging of swords;
    It is well, methinks, if the warrior meets
    A raven black on his road.

21 Another it is if out thou art come,
    And art ready forth to fare,
    To behold on the path before thy house
    Two fighters greedy of fame.

22 Third it is well if a howling wolf
    Thou hearest under the ash;
    And fortune comes if thy foe thou seest
    Ere thee the hero beholds.

23 A man shall fight not when he must face
    The moon's bright sister setting late;
    Win he shall who well can see,
    And wedge-like forms his men for the fray.

24 Foul is the sign if thy foot shall stumble
    As thou goest forth to fight;
    Goddesses baneful at both thy sides
    Will that wounds thou shalt get.

25 Combed and washed shall the wise man go,
    And a meal at morn shall take;
    For unknown it is where at eve he may be;
    It is ill thy luck to lose.

Extract from
Völsunga Saga

XX

Then said Sigurd, "Teach us the lore of mighty matters!"

She said, "Belike thou cannest more skill in all than I; yet will I teach thee; yea, and with thanks, if there be aught of my cunning that will in anywise pleasure thee, either of runes or of other matters that are the root of things; but now let us drink together, and may the Gods give to us twain a good day, that thou mayst win good help and fame from my wisdom, and that thou mayst hereafter mind thee of that which we twain speak together."

Then Brynhild filled a beaker and bore it to Sigurd, and gave him the drink of love, and spake—

> Beer bring I to thee,
> Fair fruit of the byrnies' clash,
> Mixed is it mightily,
> Mingled with fame,
> Brimming with bright lays

And pitiful runes,
Wise words, sweet words,
Speech of great game.

Runes of war know thou,
If great thou wilt be!
Cut them on hilt of hardened sword,
Some on the brand's back,
Some on its shining side,
Twice name Tyr therein.
Sea-runes good at need,
Learnt for ship's saving,
For the good health of the swimming horse;
On the stern cut them,
Cut them on the rudder-blade
And set flame to shaven oar:
Howso big be the sea-hills,
Howso blue beneath,
Hail from the main then comest thou home.

Word-runes learn well
If thou wilt that no man
Pay back grief for the grief thou gavest;
Wind thou these,
Weave thou these,
Cast thou these all about thee,
At the Thing,
Where folk throng,
Unto the full doom faring.

Of ale-runes know the wisdom
If thou wilt that another's wife
Should not bewray[1] thine heart that trusteth

---

1 Reveal.

Cut them on the mead-horn,
On the back of each hand,
And nick an N upon thy nail.

Ale have thou heed
To sign from all harm
Leek lay thou in the liquor,
Then I know for sure
Never cometh to thee,
Mead with hurtful matters mingled.

Help-runes shalt thou gather
If skill thou wouldst gain
To loosen child from low-laid mother;
Cut be they in hands hollow,
Wrapped the joints round about;
Call for the Good-folks' gainsome[2] helping.
Learn the bough-runes wisdom
If leech-lore thou lovest;
And wilt wot[3] about wounds' searching
On the bark be they scored;
On the buds of trees
Whose boughs look eastward ever.

Thought-runes shalt thou deal with
If thou wilt be of all men
Fairest-souled wight, and wisest,
These areded[4]
These first cut
These first took to heart high Hropt.

On the shield were they scored

2 Profitable.
3 Know.
4 Declared.

That stands before the shining God,
On Early-waking's ear,
On All-knowing's hoof,
On the wheel which runneth
Under Rognir's chariot;
On Sleipnir's jaw-teeth,
On the sleigh's traces.

On the rough bear's paws,
And on Bragi's tongue,
On the wolfs claws,
And on eagle's bill,
On bloody wings,
And bridge's end;
On loosing palms,
And pity's path:

On glass, and on gold,
And on goodly silver,
In wine and in wort,
And the seat of the witch-wife;
On Gungnir's point,
And Grani's bosom:
On the Norn's nail,
And the neb[5] of the night-owl.

All these so cut,
Were shaven and sheared,
And mingled in with holy mead,
And sent upon wide ways enow;[6]
Some abide with the Elves,
Some abide with the Æsir,

---

5 Beak.
6 Enough.

Or with the wise Vanir,
Some still hold the sons of mankind.

These be the book-runes,
And the runes of good help,
And all the ale-runes,
And the runes of much might;
To whomso they may avail,
Unbewildered unspoilt;
They are wholesome to have:
Thrive thou with these then.
When thou hast learnt their lore,
Till the Gods end thy life-days.

Now shalt thou choose thee
E'en as choice is bidden,
Sharp steel's root and stem,
Choose song or silence;
See to each in thy heart.
All hurt has been heeded.

Then answered Sigurd —

Ne'er shall I flee,
Though thou wottest[7] me fey;[8]
Never was I born for blenching,
Thy loved rede[9] will I
Hold aright in my heart
Even as long as I may live.

7 Know.
8 Doomed.
9 Counsel.

XXI

Sigurd spake now, "Sure no wiser woman than thou art one may be found in the wide world; yea, yea, teach me more yet of thy wisdom!"

She answers, "Seemly is it that I do according to thy will, and show thee forth more redes of great avail, for thy prayer's sake and thy wisdom;" and she spake withal—

"Be kindly to friend and kin, and reward not their trespasses against thee; bear and forbear, and win for thee thereby long enduring praise of men.

"Take good heed of evil things: a may's[10] love, and a man's wife; full oft thereof doth ill befall!

"Let not thy mind be overmuch crossed by unwise men at thronged meetings of folk; for oft these speak worse than they wot of; lest thou be called a dastard, and art minded to think that thou art even as is said; slay such an one on another day, and so reward his ugly talk.

"If thou farest by the way whereas bide evil things, be well ware of thyself; take not harbour near the highway, though thou be benighted, for oft abide there ill wights for men's bewilderment.

"Let not fair women beguile thee, such as thou mayst meet at the feast, so that the thought thereof stand thee instead of sleep, and a quiet mind; yea, draw them not to thee with kisses or other sweet

10 Maiden's.

things of love.

"If thou hearest the fool's word of a drunken man, strive not with him being drunk with drink and witless; many a grief, yea, and the very death, groweth from out such things.

"Fight thy foes in the field, nor be burnt in thine house.

"Never swear thou wrongsome oath; great and grim is the reward for the breaking of plighted troth.

"Give kind heed to dead men—sick-dead, sea-dead, or sword-dead; deal needfully with their dead corpses.

"Trow[11] never in him for whom thou hast slain father, brother, or whatso near kin, yea, though young he be; *for oft waxes wolf in youngling*.

"Look thou with good heed to the wiles of thy friends; but little skill is given to me, that I should foresee the ways of thy life; yet good it were that hate fell not on thee from those of thy wife's house."

Sigurd spake, "None among the sons of men can be found wiser than thou; and thereby swear I, that thee will I have as my own, for near to my heart thou liest."

She answers, "Thee would I fainest[12] choose, though I had all men's sons to choose from."

And thereto they plighted troth both of them.

---

11 Trust.
12 Be most inclined to.

Ancient Saws
and Proverbs

1   A man's own hand is most to be trusted. (iv)

2   Pride and wrong often end badly. (vii)

3   The nights of blood[1] are the nights of most impatience. (ix)

4   The cattle are like their master. (xiii)

5   Nothing venture, nothing have. (v)

6   Ill goes it with those who are born on a barren[2] land. (vi)

7   Be warned by another's woe. (xiii)

8   I shall let another's wound be my warning. (xxxvii)

9   His hands are clean who warns another. (xli)

10   But a short while is [the] hand fain of[3] [the] blow. (xlii)

11   Slow and sure. (xliv)

---

1 The very night one is wronged.
2 Foreign.
3 Pleased with. ("The hour of victory is short.")

12   Ill redes[4] bring ill luck. (xlv)

13   'Tis the turn of mind of all men first to give away what has been stolen, if they have it in their keeping. (xlix)

14   Birds of a feather flock most together. (li)

15   Never break the peace which good men and true make between thee and others. (lv)

16   With law shall our land be built up and settled, and with lawlessness wasted and spoiled. (lxix)

17   Never cheat thy master. (lxxxvi)

18   No tree falls at the first stroke. (xcix)

19   Ill seed has been sown, and so an ill crop will spring from it. (cxiv)

20   Those live long who are slain with words alone. (cxlv)

21   Wolves eat another's message. (xxiii)

22   A bird in the hand [is] better than two in the bush. (xxiv)

23   High tides are best for hale.[5] (xl)

24   One fool in every stock.[6] (liii)

25   Braver are many in word than in deed. (iv)

26   The friend aye warns his friend of ill. (xiv)

---

4 Counsels.
5 Happy signs.
6 Breed.

27   He knoweth most who most hath tried. (xiv)

28   'Tis ill to rouse a hasty temper. (xiv)

29   Many seem wise who are lacking in wit. (xiv)

30   The thrall alone takes instant vengeance, the coward never. (xv)

31   Alone in misfortune is worst. (xvi)

32   Work not done needs no reward. (xvii)

33   Many a trifle happens at eve. (xviii)

34   Everyone is master of his own words. (xix)

35   Ale is another man.[7] (xix)

36   Long shall a man be tried. (xx)

37   The guess of the wise is truth. (xxxi)

38   Luck is one thing, brave deeds another. (xxxiv)

39   Men will tell of deeds that are done. (xl)

40   No man shapes his own fortune. (xli)

41   The over-praised are the worst deceivers. (xlv)

42   One man's tale is but half a tale. (xlvi)

43   There is more in the heart of man than money can buy. (xlvii)

44   One evil is mended by a worse one. (xlviii)

7 ("A man is different when drunk than when sober.")

45 Many have been brought to death by over-confidence. (liv)

46 Ill is the lot of him who has an ill name. (lvi)

47 Oft in the woods is a listener nigh. (lix)

48 The fire is hottest to him who is in it. (lix)

49 The unjust man prospers ill. (lxii)

50 Trust no man so well that you trust not yourself better. (lxvii)

51 The hand turns to its wonted[8] skill, and that which we have learned in youth is always most familiar to us. (lxxviii)

52 Many go to the goat-house to get wool. (lxxviii)

53 There are few more certain tokens of evil than not to know how to accept the good. (lxxviii)

54 Old friends are the last to break away. (lxxxii)

55 It is ill to have a thrall for your friend. (lxxxii)

56 Bare is his back who has no brother. (lxxxii)

57 No man is a fool if he keeps silence. (lxxxviii)

58 All good things are in threes. (lxxxviii)

59 No blame is borne by those who warn. (iv)

60 Those who fulfil their vows never come to grief. (vi)

---

8 Usual.

61   Seldomer should we have to regret that which we say too little than that which we say too much. (vii)

62   Know one thing, know thyself. (vii)

63   That is why ye young men never come to aught, that you flinch at all things. (vii)

64   People often do by chance things worse than they would.[9] (x)

65   'Tis not my curse what's common fate. (x)

66   Ye will have something for your pertinacity— either some comfort, or otherwise a humiliation still greater than before. (x)

67   Short is the age of over-boldness. (xiv)

68   One grows craven as one grows old. (xvii)

69   A wise counsel do I deem it to come to peace. (xx)

70   It will only come to evil if folk will be casting words of shame at each other. (xx)

71   By wise men [distance] was deemed most like to allay their rage. (xx)

72   Oft is a fiend in a fair skin. (xvi)

73   Many become brave when brought to bay,[10] but natheless are not over-brave between whiles. (xviii)

---

9 Intend.
10 When in dire straits.

74   It is good to have two mouths for the two kinds of speech. (xvi)

75   Many a man keeps his word of foster-brothership but middlingly well. (xvi)

76   It is better to keep one's promise. (xix)

77   Varied will be his fortunes who fares far. (vi)

78   That alone is seemly, to hold truly to troth[11] given. (iv)

79   All men [must] need die, and from that season shall none escape. (v)

80   Sweet to [the] eye while seen. (v)

81   No might 'gainst many. (xi)

82   Many a man lives after hope has grown little. (xii)

83   Whoso comes amongst many shall one day find that no one man is by so far the mightiest of all. (xviii)

84   Whenas men meet foes in fight, better is stout heart than sharp sword. (xix)

85   Where wolf's ears are, wolf's teeth are near. (xix)

86   Ill life to sit lamenting for what we may not have. (xxiv)

11 Loyalty.

87 Who shall say what goodhap[12] folk may bear
    to their life's end? (xxiv)

88 Ill [it is] to abash folk of their mirth. (xv)

89 Good to love good things when all goes
    according to thy heart's desire. (xxviii)

90 Never nourish thou a wolfcub. (xxx)

91 Seldom hath hardy eld[13] a faint-heart youth.
    (xviii)

92 Who can't defend the wealth they have must
    die, or share with the rover brave. (vi)

93 The commonalty always loves what is new.
    (xxxiii)

94 It is their lot who follow kings that they
    enjoy high honours, and are more respected
    than other men, but stand often in danger
    of their lives. (lxvii)

95 Everyone has some friend even among his
    enemies. (lxxiii)

96 It is not a less honourable condition to be
    in the number of bondes,[14] and have one's
    words free. (lxxix)

97 There are few things for which you cannot
    find a match. (lxxxvi)

---

12 Happy. ("Who can say what sorrow carefree folk carry with them
to death?")
13 Old age.
14 To be counted among servants.

98   It is not wonderful[15] that luck should accompany understanding. (cxxxi)

99   A rotten branch will be found in every tree. (cxlviii)

100   My own hand is the truest test. (cliii)

101   Two masters at a time were one too many. (clxx)

102   Eagles should show their claws, though dying. (clxxxvi)

103   Kinsmen to kinsmen should be true. (clxxxvi)

104   Short is the hour for acting, and long the hour for feasting. (xxviii)

105   To take up great resolutions, and then to lay them aside, would only end in dishonour. (IX)

106   The king has many ears. (lxxxix)

107   What people wish they soon believe. (cxxii)

108   With many who come to power and honour, pride keeps pace with promotion. (viii)

109   The sluggard waits till afternoon. (xvii)

110   Childhood is hasty. (xxvii)

111   It is an old custom for the wisest to give way. (xxvii)

112   Numbers cannot skill withstand. (lxv)

---

15 Surprising.

113 Bravery is half victory. (civ)

114 Bad counsel comes to a bad end. (vi)

115 End a stout life by death as stout. (vi)

116 One whose life you save [often] gives none, or a very bad return. (xxi)

117 Sorrow is lightened by being brought out openly. (xviii)

118 He will be avenged who falls forward.[16] (xxiv)

119 'Tis good to drive home with your wain[17] whole. (xxxviii)

120 Many farings, many fortunes. (xxxviii)

121 All should be told to a friend. (lvi)

122 He falls not whom true friends help forward on his way. (lxvii)

123 He must tend the oak who is to dwell beneath it. (lxxi)

124 [A] son's place to his sire another son born alone can fill. (lxxxi)

125 Oft comes ill from women's gossip. (vi)

126 Brothers' goods are fairest to look on when they lie together.[18] (vi)

127 Gift answers to gift, you know, and one hand washes the other. (ix)

---

16 Who dies bravely.
17 Wagon.
18 ("One should share with kin.")

128 Women's counsel is always unlucky. (x)

129 Fee[19] is best for a fey[20] man. (xvi)

130 There are no foes like those of one's own house. (xvi)

131 That were ill counselled to lend one's money to unknown men. (vii)

132 Long we remember what youth gained us. (xiii)

133 Eyes will betray if maid love man. (xiii)

134 Things go by turns. (xxxi)

135 Age cows a man. (xlvi)

136 Prove it by trial, and take it not on hearsay of others. (ii)

137 Folk's eyes are apt at squinting toward money. (vi)

138 Words will not slay me. (vi)

139 Evilly the thing began, and in likewise shall end. (viii)

140 Best but to hear of woeful thanes.[21] (viii)

141 A man's foes are those of his own house.[22] (viii)

---

19 A bribe.
20 Doomed.
21 ("It is best to know wicked men only by hearsay.")
22 ("The worst blows come from your own kin.")

142 [Do] not aid a man who has slain his liege lord. (vi)

143 [Do] not protect a man who has slain one of his comrades. (vi)

144 [Your] wife ought not to be always leaving home to visit her relatives. (vi)

145 [You] ought not to stay out late with your sweetheart. (vi)

146 [Do] not ride your best horse when in a hurry. (vi)

147 [You] ought not to bring up[23] the child of a man in a better position. (vi)

148 Always be cheerful towards one who comes for hospitality. (vi)

149 Never lay Tyrfing[24] on the ground. (vi)

150 [Do not] tell secrets to your sweetheart. (viii)

23 Chasten.
24 Your sword.

Sources and Editions

Havamal, Sigrdrifumol, and Reginsmol

Poetic Edda. Translated by Henry Adams Bellows. New York: The American-Scandinavian Foundation, 1923.

Völsunga Saga

The Volsunga Saga translated From the Icelandic. Translated by Eirikr Magnusson and William Morris. London: Norrœna Society, 1907.

Ancient Saws and Proverbs

The *Ancient Saws and Proverbs* in this collection overlap significantly with the modern collection called *Sögumál*, which the compiler describes as "wisdom inspired by and from the Icelandic Sagas"—this is a collection of 251 sayings, many of which are not drawn from any text but are paraphrases, interpolations, and rephrasings.

The 150 sayings in the present collection are taken directly from textual sources, editions of which are cited below. The order in which they are presented roughly follows *Sögumál* for comparative purposes, but many sayings included here are not present in *Sögumál*, and most of those from *Völsunga Saga* are contained in the section excerpted from ch. xx–xxi.

In some cases, sayings have been altered to address the reader rather than as indirect speech between characters; e.g. no. 142, the original being related by Heithrek's father to his mother, "he must not aid a man who has slain his liege lord". Changes are indicated by square brackets. Each saying is followed by the chapter number of its respective work in parentheses.

1–4: Viga Glum's Saga

Viga-Glum's Saga. The story of Viga-Glum. Translated by Sir Edmund Head. Williams and Norgate: 1866.

5–20: Njal's Saga

The story of Burnt Njal; from the Icelandic of the Njals Saga. Translated by George Webbe Dasent. London: Grant Richards, 1900.

21–24: Laxdæla Saga

The story of the Laxdalers done into English. Translated by Robert Proctor. London: Charles Whittingham & Company, 1903

25–58: Grettir's Saga

The saga of Grettir the Strong; a story of the eleventh century. Translated by George Ainslie Hight. London: J. M. Dent, 1913.

59–68: Hrafnkels Saga

Summer traveling in Iceland; being the narrative of two journeys across the island by unfrequented routes. Translated by J. M. Coles. London: John Murray, 1882.

69–71: Heidarviga Saga

72–73: Eyrbyggja Saga

The Saga Library Vol. II: The Story of the Ere-Dwellers with the Story of the Heath-Slayings as Appendix. Translated by William Morris and Eiríkr Magnússon. London: Bernard Quaritch, 1892.

74–76: Saga of Thorstein Viking's Son

77: Saga of Frithjof the Bold

Viking Tales of the North. The Sagas of Thorstein, Viking's Son, and Frithjof the Bold. Translated by Rasmus B. Anderson. Chicago: S. C. Griggs and Co., 1877.

78–91: Völsunga Saga

The Volsunga Saga translated From the Icelandic. Translated by Eirikr Magnusson and William Morris. London: Norrœna Society, 1907.

92–103: Saga of Olaf Haraldsson

104: Saga of Hakon the Good

105–107: Olaf Trygvisson's Saga

108–109: Saga of Magnus the Good

110–113: Saga of Harald Hardrade

114–116: Saga of Magnus Barefoot

117: Saga of Sigurd the Crusader and His Brothers Eystein and Olaf

The Heimskringla or Sagas of the Norse Kings, from the Icelandic of Snorre Sturlason, Vols. I–IV. Translated by Samuel Laing. London: John C. Nimmo, 1889.

118–124: Egil's Saga

The story of Egil Skallagrimsson : being an Icelandic family history of the ninth and tenth centuries. Translated by W. C. Green. London: E. Stock, 1893.

125–130: Gisli Sursson's Saga

The Story of Gisli the Outlaw. Translated by George Webbe Dasent. Philadelphia: J. B. Lippincott and Co., 1866.

131–133: Tale of Gunnlaug the Worm-tongue and Raven the Skald

The story of Gunnlaug the Worm-tongue and Raven the Skald. Translated by William Morris. London: Chiswick Press, 1891.

134–135: Saga of Thrond of Gate

The Tale of Thrond of Gate: Commonly Called Faereyinga Saga. Translated by F. York Powell. London: David Nutt, 1896.

136–137: Bandamanna Saga

138–141: Hen-Thorir's Saga

The Story of Howard the Halt; the story of the banded men; the story of Hen Thorir. Translated by William Morris and Eiríkr Magnússon. London: Bernard Quaritch, 1891.

142–150: Saga of Hervör and Heidrek

Stories and Ballads of the Far Past. Translated by N. Kershaw. Cambridge University Press, 1921.

Studies in Reaction Series:

9 781922 602541